A JILLION MUSINGS

Akanksha Negi

BookLeaf Publishing

India | USA | UK

Presentation by *BookLeaf Publishing*

Web: www.bookleafpub.com

E-mail: info@bookleafpub.com

ISBN: 9789363308947

First edition 2024

To my dearest 'Vardaan'..

You might not be physically here with me.

But know this, our love transcends the realms of earth and also heaven..

For it cannot be measured in distance and time

Wherever you are, you will always be mine

For ours is a bond that time will only strengthen..

Chronicle of Moments

The pregnancy was going smooth, until it wasn't...

The dawn of 12th June 2024 brings quiet
alarm—subtle shifts stir the air.
A journey to the emergency room—a decision is
made.
One hour later, my son arrives.
A soul in distress.

Yet his breath is shallow, his cries hushed by the
weight of his struggle.
A new path begins, marked by tubes and whispers
of fragility.
In the NICU, he battles shadows—against
infection, against silence.
Hope rises, though delicate—talks of discharge
flicker like a distant star.

Day 14
The scales tip once more. All efforts seem
exhausted, the doctors' voices hollow with
uncertainty.
The struggle deepens, and even faith seems to
wane.
A soul fights, but the odds grow heavier with each
passing breath.

D- Day, 28th June 2024

Baby becomes immortal, set free from his
sufferings.
Life as I knew, ends.
World shattered.

ACKNOWLEDGEMENT

This entire venture wouldn't have been possible without the support of my family and friends, especially my husband, Anchit, who is my absolute rock and forever companion through the ebbs and flows of life. A special shoutout to my firstborn—Yashwin, you may be very small right now but you have been my biggest source of strength and willpower.

These are the people who believed in my way of healing myself and gave me the space and time to breathe and take a moment.

I am also indebted to 'BookLeaf Publishing' who gave me this wonderful platform and opportunity to let me express and restore myself creatively and constructively.

Writing when feeling alone or sad might not be everyone's solution, but it certainly has worked for me and helped me be a better version of myself in these trying times.

PREFACE

Trigger Warning

A baby's death, what does it do to a mother?

She keeps the baby safe and sound only to lose him in a matter of a few weeks.

What do you say to a grieving mother, to make her feel better? How do you tell her that she will not have any future moments with her child, that each day not only does she have to deal with the pain of losing but also learn to live without that baby for all the years to come.

You don't say anything—for you do not have the emotional quotient to fathom that loss. You give her space, a shoulder to cry on, you listen to her grieve and when she feels the slightest bit 'normal' you tell her that she did a great job with the baby and no other person could show such insurmountable courage in the face of such an episode. You tell her that she was the best mother the baby could have. Most importantly, let your actions show that you care for her!

This set of poems captures the myriad of emotions I felt in these past few months. With the written word and my experience I have tried my best to normalise emotions and issues one feels while navigating loss, especially related to the taboo that is prevalent around losing your baby. There is still a lot of unnecessary stigma attached to it in our "progressive" society and is hardly given any importance and emotional support, which not only aggravates a grieving mother but delays her recovery from such a traumatic incident.

Hoping my poems positively leave an impression on all who read, whether you're the one who has had to deal with any loss, miscarriage or know of anyone who has, you can come out with a better clarity of this tumultuous journey and be more empathetic.

Not all days are bad, some are very bad. But then there are few moments where you see why you're alive and you don't want to just live, you want to thrive.

Whoever you are, I see you, I feel for you, you are not alone, we are in this together.

Just us Two

The night lamp fills the corner with a warm
glow
me and you lying in the bed, just us two
the noises from outside simply drown
the second I start gazing at you..

I look at you, my baby as you dream asleep,
your chest going high and low
there's nowhere I'd rather be, nowhere I'd rather
go
what did I do to deserve this pleasure

My heart completely full, I slide towards you,
even though you're inches away cannot keep my
hands off you.
We don't know what the future holds for us
but these moments I will always treasure.

Wishing this, what we have here never ends
my brain and heart forget how life with you
before was
gently stroking your forehead, I see you smile,
mummy's here, mummy's near, my sweet little
boy, you're forever mine.

Practice Gratitude

We're taught to be grateful, say 'please', say 'thank you',
practice gratitude, they say, a smile goes a long way...
these values are long forgotten
Can we go back to our innocence—no-one has a clue

Always reminding the children, to appreciate the small things
But do we do the same? I dare say…
Is it only about the number of battles we've won?
As grownups, we're constantly living with a hint of blue..

Only worrying about superficial things, we cut
our own wings
Living life chaotically ever ready to jump the
gun
Ignoring countless emotions and gestures, we
lose track
Growing older, learning to live, cut yourselves
some slack!

With our never-ending wish list, the ambition
knows no bounds
Wear this, get that, go there, eat here, vices bang
on the stack..
If we don't keep up, there is fear of missing out
People easily fall into depression, it's indeed as
bad as it sounds.

Does it always take a jolt—an accident, death or
sickness to wake one up?
Stop and take notice—a child that smiles, a
stranger that holds the door
Plenty of niceness around, I have no doubt.
Find beauty in the setting sun or divinity in a full
moon—
Surely there is another way of looking at life's
cup.

Once you're woke, all redundant garbage won't
matter

No arguments, materialistic desires,
suddenly the soul has so much more breathing
room—
the mind begins to drown the superfluous patter.

But how long will you last in this zone
Don't wait for another episode to appreciate this
boon
What doesn't kill you only makes you stronger
So hopefully only one judder is enough to
realise,
gratitude is bound to make you live longer.

Why Me

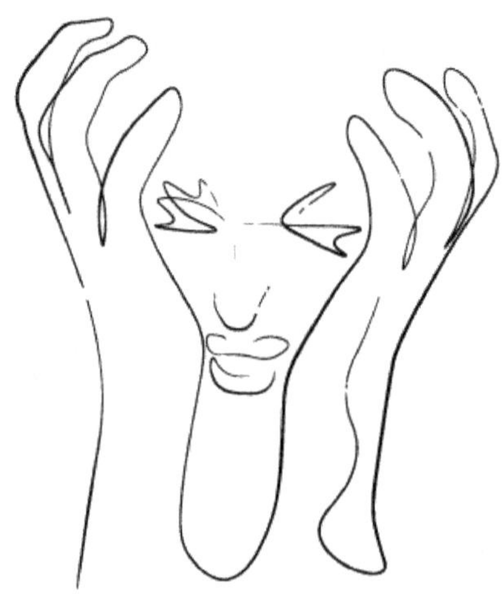

Everything that happens, happens for a reason
A popular belief amongst many
If you got what you wanted—you deserved it!
If things went south—something better is bound
to happen
Just wait for a better season

Incidents happen, people move on
But the one most affected, has a tough climb on
When the storm passes and the dust settles
A question often comes back to the victims
Why me?

Was it my ill intention, something I did a million
years ago
Now that I am the one being punished
I must face the music and go with the flow
For this too shall pass and I will eventually be
guilt-free
Or will it forever be 'why me?'

How can she do it, I would have died
This circumstance seems devastating, I would
have barely survived
Such critique is typical from everyone you know
O dear friend, do not try to put yourself in my
shoes
For we must bear our own burdens

You cannot possibly do it, like I can't face your
woes
It's funny how we are custom built to navigate
our own lows.
Stand with me and give me a smile
I am built for this, just need some time
The question still faintly lingers—'why me?'

Time passes and the thinking evolves
You are proud enough to wear your battle scar
For the war is far from over, self-doubt dissolves
Why you, the answer is just sublime
'cause it could only be done by you, the star.

Losing You

It was supposed to be one of my happiest days
But, cruel fate, couldn't keep its claws away
It crept, leapt and swept what was mine
I fought hard but couldn't win over the devious
swine

Eyes welling up with a thousand tears
How much can one cry..
I feel a perennial lump stuck in my throat;
thoughts awry
All bad elements becoming true, my worst fears!

Tough to close the eyes, without their last
moments flashing by..
Is that all I can think of? I want to die
Emotional pain presents itself physically too
Head bursting with their echoes, can't escape but
you can try

Finding yourself randomly bursting into tears is
common
Never know what may trigger you even in the
middle of obvious fun
Mood changes in a second and you start bawling
In a bottomless pit you often find yourself
falling

Bright lights appear sharp, as though poking
holes
Darkness becomes your friend, its teeth in you
full of hate
Optimism goes out the window and remorse
enters the gate
You try and get back to routine for there are
other roles also at play

You don't seek them, their memories find a way
to you
Grief is more paralysing than fear
It comes discounted with no expiration date

Can stay fresh as a lily though colossal in
weight.

Grief manifests itself differently each day,
Always a step ahead of you
Breathing down your neck and intimidating you
out of the blue
Ever reminding of the loss which is here to stay.

Losing you is the hardest thing I do everyday.

Lost in Translation

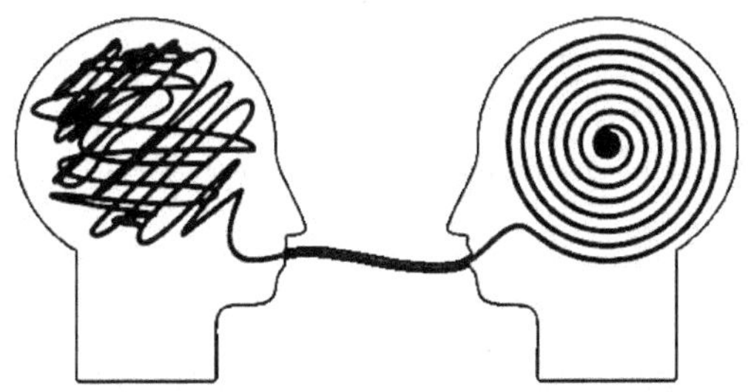

Through the written word, will try my best to get
to you
What it's like—the trauma and pain
I will tell you all about it again and again
But I am afraid it will all be lost in translation

I don't blame you, if you can't empathise the
way I want
For it's only me who has to bear the brunt
forever over and over again
For the more I talk about it the better I feel
Perhaps, it's the only way my mind and soul will
heal

What he meant to me, and where I am now
Don't be a stranger but just ask me why and how
I will tell you everything all over again
But I am afraid it will all be lost in translation

How do I explain something that is so abstract
You never met him, never bonded how can I
expect you to feel any impact
Whatever you understand is all 'cause of your
love for me
It's me who you worry about, you want to set me
free

I wish you could help me the way you want to
And I wish I could express myself in a way that
you'd understand
Such is the ugliness of this circumstance nothing
we do alleviates the pain
I am afraid it is all lost in translation

If only I could show my feelings to you
How I felt the touch, the sounds and what it did
to me
how my heart smiled with him, full of glee
How can I portray when it's meant to be felt,
fully understood by just a few

So, don't run away from me
Even if these are uncharted roads for you, I
appreciate you trying
Tread lightly and let me be, and smile for me
even if I am crying
I can try describing again—but I am afraid it
will be lost in translation.

No pity, Please!

Yes, something bad happened nay 'twas tragic
suddenly, my life seems dull without magic.
Where did all the happiness disappear,
it was here just seconds ago

Your intentions are great, but they fill me with
contempt and rage
as though all my life up till now deserves no
value.
For I am only judged by this brutal episode of
fate
"It only came into your life to take what was
due," sad remarks cue

This occurrence made my soul graduate, leaving
my body demoted

with whatever little control, I raised my arms to
surrender.
Your ways to comfort me, inadvertently pulling
me down
the constant pity, turns my smile into a frown

While I look back and see courage and pride
your sympathy corners me to one side.
All emotions I have felt since, be it joy or
sorrow, now amplified
whereas you give me pity eyes, like I have
barely survived

Look at me from a novel perspective
I am trying to champion grief and loss
Why do you keep comparing me with who I was
and what I lost,
the life-lessons it has taught me are very
subjective

I had an identity before this too
And would want you to see me without the
perennial sympathy
Life happens, today it's me and god forbid it
ever be you
My loss has opened me to view things
differently, not with apathy

Yes, I have lost a piece of my soul and can never
return to whole
But also received new virtues, that I would like
to proudly wear
Has there ever been a gain without any rough
use and tear?
I want you to see me and my grit, not what I
have lost and my heart's hole

I am trying to move on and go back to living
carefree
The loss is uncovering a new and stronger
version of the old me
You may not know what to say
"I'm so sorry for you" repeating this every time
just isn't the right way.

What could have been

I close my eyes trying to sleep
And first thing that flashes is you next to me
your intoxicating smell and soft touch
Is it really happening, or I have nothing as such

Eyes now open, I stare expressionless above
No one holding me gently, just me and my
thoughts
Of what could have been, if only you were here
I'd have no reason to dream about my loss

My ears will forever long to hear your first
words,

eyes will forever search you in the beauty of this
earth,
lips will long to feel your soft skin
nose will have to do without your scent, for
nothing is akin.

Rocking you to sleep and then looking at you for
hours,
Dressing you up everyday, dousing you with
love till you smelt like flowers
Walking with you in the stroller, doing
everything together
Is now just a faint desire, to fall true, it will take
more than forever

Our magical hugs, activities under the sun, not
to forget bedtime fun,
Oh, the life we could have had, all things said
and done.
It wasn't what I wanted but what God had in
mind
We may plan it all, but in the end, it's just what
we wish for or actual moments in time

I miss all our firsts that I looked forward to,
Have to make do with only the lasts I had, and
know will have nothing new
It's not the most ideal of situations to keep
dreaming of you

But I often see myself rewinding the times we
had, no matter how few.

Given a choice—to go through it again or to
erase you from my memories
my mind says to erase while my heart begs to
live it in a loop
For it was when you were alive and I was
complete, pictures full in my galleries.
In life, you never know who is taken off-stage,
no matter how prepared to jump the hoop!

Thinking about years down the line, no matter
how things unfold
What could have been—will I tell every kid
about you or will you be a story untold?
I might not miss the baby but will think of the
man you could have become
my soul would have had no holes, sometimes
life seems better when so humdrum

We have a special bond and for eternity it will
stay
Your memories are tough to keep but tougher to
give away
And as I make peace with what I have knowing
reminiscing is not a sin,
in the corner of my mind, I still wonder—what
could have been…

They said

Nurses coming in and doing their thing
not addressing the elephant in the room,
an empty crib next to a new mother's bed
Surely they're used to it, but for me, it was the
beginning of the end.

Did they not see? It's enough to tie anyone's
tongue in a knot
Some make eye contact, others choose to not
Touching shoulders, caressing hair, without
saying a word.
Are all ways to show you care, but rather not be
heard.

"Pull yourself together, be brave…"
they said

while their own lips trembling, eyes looking
grave.
I just lost a piece of my soul, courage hanging
by a thread.

"Keep yourself busy…"
they said, is it ever easy?
Why do you want me to jump from one thing to
another
Let me process this, after all, I was his mother.

"This will make you stronger…." they said
I'd rather have my baby than be a powerhouse of
strength
For what use is this virtue to me?
Right now I'm at my weakest, can't you see?

"You never know the issues you could have had
with him in future…."
They said
Should I thank my stars whilst holding my
painful suture?
If only I could get more time with him, have no
desire to skip ahead.

"I don't know why this happened to you, you're
such a kind person…."
They said

Maybe it only happens to saints or humans who
have a good heart
Or it's just that life happens and seldom you're
untimely pulled apart

"It's what God wanted, something better will
come…."
they said.
But what about right now?
Why am I made to suffer for the promise of a
better tomorrow and how!

"Plan again, if it's meant to be it will happen
again…"
they said.
I don't know if I can go through the ten months
again with no certainty
Months might fly for others, but to me will seem
like eternity.

"Count your blessing, life has been so good to
you,"
They said
Then why retrospectively I'd look back and this
day I will rue.
If I didn't want this pitfall, should I have quit
while ahead?

"Can you tell what exactly happened,"
They said
learn the do's and don'ts once you hear such
tragic news about someone you know
'cause everyone wants to be warned and save
themselves from a similar blow

People around me are all wired differently
Some handle it head on and others with a tad
difficulty
It's fascinating to see how different beliefs and
similar notes emerge for one outcome
Like if the fruit is spoken as 'tomato', it's
"tomaato" for some.

The way you see Her

Everyone is dealt a different hand, sometimes
it's good and sometimes bad
You might be having the best day, somewhere
your friend would be sad
You want to help her, she might need you too
It's a bit complex as you don't want her to feel
odd with you.

How would it be with her?
Will you mask your happiness to accommodate
her grief?
Or will she fake her mood and with you be brief.
Can be neither, she may just need your smile and
a spur.

You want to laugh out loud, but she might listen
and feel bad, you fear?

Don't walk on eggshells and let the sounds die
down when she's near.
She has already forgotten how to sway to the
tune
and has had everything come crashing down on
her in the month of June.

You might feel the air is heavy in her presence
It's just a testimony to her circumstance that was
so intense
Air will be diffused with your optimism and be
lighter
For you are starting to see your friend in the
right light and she is a fighter.

You may right now have all that she desires and
needs
But your love will make her stand strong, even
in the weeds.
Don't be afraid to celebrate, happiness increases
when you share
Goes to show, you want her in your life and how
much you care.

She has already lost so much,
Would hate to lose the intimacy, just be her
crutch
And she will dance in your happiness more than
you

For you are a friend to her, part of her crew.

Yes, there will be times when she will be
reminded of her loss
Getting over someone's absence is to make a
cactus gloss
But she could never project her longings on
anyone else's life
She values her relationships too much to cause
any strife.

Never stepping in the same river twice, you are
ever-growing
Though you may take 3 steps forward and 1 step
back, without knowing.
Deal with her separately, as her trauma is a
forced handout by Lord,
How you see her, is maybe how she will start to
see herself coming out of this fjord.

As they say, the show must go on,
You are here only for a few moments before you
are long gone
So don't waste time trying to navigate these
flows
Enjoy your friends and try and make them forget
their woes

Friendship is a two-way street, you reap what
you sow
She will be there for you as much as you express
and show
Everyone comes with their own emotional
baggage and might drag them to places afar
Not all who suffer will make you hold their bags
of grief but maybe just one jar.

The ties that lift

More than 8 billion people on this earth
Looking left or right, crowds everywhere, there
is no dearth
From all those beating hearts
Why is it that you get pulled only to a few
Doesn't matter whether they're old or brand
new.

You may not talk all day everyday
Sometimes when together, might even have
nothing to say.
These ties go beyond the physical realm
Come stormy weather in the oceans of your
mind
They will be your anchors and keep you from
drifting, one of a kind.

These invisible bonds keep us sane,
in our moments of madness, alleviate our pain.
To you, their company feels nothing out of the
ordinary.
There's just something about the vibe they give,
you may just be surviving but they show you
how to live.

Not like they have got nothing better to do,
love in these ties is just so pure and true.
You are a priority for them.
You can see it in their actions, even society
knows how much you care.
Try pretending in front of them, you will be
called-out, I dare!

You don't have to make an effort or think twice
before speaking
It's a judgement-free zone, you get the comfort
you're seeking
Is it a game of numbers, how many such do you
need?
If it's true friendship then even one will do
If not, then even a swarm of "friends" can't pull
you out of the deepest blue.

No one is equipped to handle your losses and
grief,
but they listen and help you turn over a new leaf.

Prior experience doesn't count, only compassion
and empathy.
These friends spread their angelic wings and
take you under their aegis
Keeping you safe from unnecessary comments
of the world and preaches.

Don't know what would happen if I were to face
my hardships alone?
For my ties help me heal in mind, body and soul.
Why so much stress on ties, you ask!
You may think that's what spouses are for,
But how can they fix you, if they're broken too
and are still sore.

There's nothing that unites better than facing
trauma together
Such pits in your life show you who're here to
stay now and forever
The ties move on from one life to the next
Souls recognizing and respecting each other no
matter what,
such lifting ties are earned by good deeds and
can't be bought.

Finding her wings

Where is she, cannot find her
I call her name but no answer, only
echoes—alas!
Is she trying another door, everything is such a
blur
Her feeble attempt to escape this house of
broken glass.

Torn and tattered, bruised and battered, can see
right through the holes
Darkness engulfing every little of her light, true
to its form.
Time flies by, you see her, dragging herself on
her hurt soles

she is not what she used to be, wings severely
damaged in the storm.

The luck of the draw destroys her chance at the
life of everyone's dream,
How can she stand up straight, shoulders pulled
back, head held high
she cannot grasp why she is unable to do
anything, her spirit so low.
Looking around she sees her reflection in all
eyes—pity, hope becoming lean

She closes her eyes and takes account of her loss
The Gods take pity and whisper words of
courage in her ear
Her soul may be bent out of shape, a cross she
has to bear
Eyes now open she sees the world in a different
light, full of rage devoid of fear.

Why this anger, this desire to annihilate, she
thinks
If ever the world had to end, let it erupt today 3,
2, 1…Boom?
Will it bring her baby back or the calm lost in
the last few months anytime soon?
Moping over it won't do any good, she has to
mentally break the jinx

She smiled and slowly felt the wounds heal
Wings patching up with gold, only the brave get
threads of this shade
She dreams of soaring higher, a place where her
holes slowly begin to seal
Turning warm with optimism, the pitch black
within her begins to fade

Like a fledgling, peeping from the edge of the
cliff
Seeing the height, the rocky shore and the deep
water that lies below
She looks behind to see her loved ones, all
huddled up with a gaze all stiff
Can she dare to take the flight again, trauma and
pain making her slow.

With no harness she takes off, leaping into
nothing, the icy air stings
Finding it hard to flap, evidently missing the
rhythm to sustain herself in the air
She soon realises—the only way is up and with
that dusts the rust off her groaning wings
Dodging raindrop pellets again, struggling to
stay afloat, she thinks how is this fair?

You may fall, but you dare not flinch,
Flying is what you were born to do, so go own
the sky and do it any other way

Everything in this life, comes with a salty pinch
Learn to savour the flavour, taste everything, and
you will forever seize the day.

What next?

You get up in the morning, fresh as a lily,
A brand new day, or is it?
Or you simply chose to sleep your woes away.
Mornings are for affirmations, but it seems
harder to keep faith.

Maybe dressing up will make you feel better,
It's merely a common way to fool your brain
Stuffing yourself mindlessly to pass time away
You don't know the person who you were
before—so driven, a go-getter.

Where's the spirit to focus and be productive?
This setback has changed the way you function
You think hard and say, what next? But, without
gumption.

It's a contrasting path than what you had
imagined.

You want to appear aloof while make changes
around,
To feel more in control, have a say,
But what's meant to happen will happen any
other way.
Getting harder and harder to look at the bigger
picture seeing the reality on the ground.

Where do you go from here?
Can dreams and desires be changed in a blink of
an eye
Or can you go back to your old life, it won't
happen but you can try
You can attempt to make new plans, but if they
too fail then 'what next?'

Your body feels like it has aged 100 years
For now it knows no next…
How can you possibly transition from where you
are?
The closer you get to happiness, your trauma
makes it seem far

Will you be able to give your 100 percent to
others in this life, no matter the bend

They don't constantly deserve your restlessness
and mood swings
When will the giving stop, they too should be on
the receiving end.
Even they end up asking in their minds—'What
next?'

Do you give up on excitement and celebrating
small wins?
Or every time you reach any milestone in life,
you start recalling your sins.
Every time you pray for something, you don't
know what you will eventually get.
You are silently dreading the 'what if' that often
precedes the 'what next'.

A moment of separation

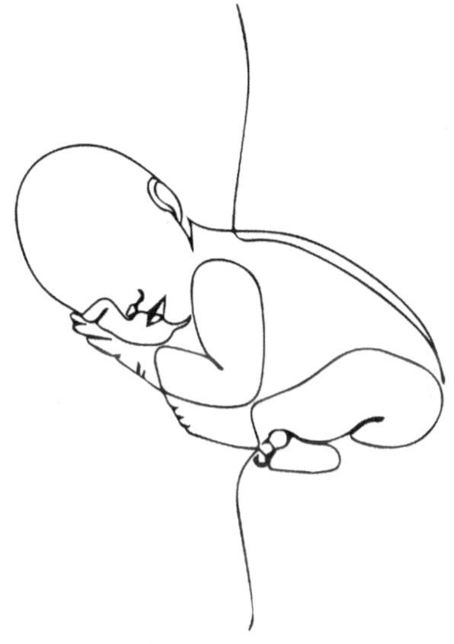

My hands tremble as I write this, eyes welling
up
reliving that damned moment, is like walking
limbless uphill.
When the earth stopped spinning, happiness
dropped dead,
for it couldn't match the whirling going inside
my head.
Didn't know words too could kill.

The doctor's speech fell flat on my ears,
only to bounce from a million objects,

bolting to pierce me with repeated hits.
My strength and energy felt scattered around the
room,
enough to detonate my body into a billion bits

My brain told me to stay calm, it said "you will
live through this"
Legs felt lifeless, like they could no longer bear
my own weight.
Heart slowing down, each beat seemed to
eventuate every hour.
Stomach left in knots, as though I rode on a
1000 rollercoaster all at once
And my poor heart wailed in a frequency that
could make one deaf, near or far.

I just saw you literally minutes ago
How can a goodbye for now be on the cards
I refuse to accept the reality that is about to go
down.
This is not what I had planned for us,
Living my worst nightmare, dreams sinking, all
hope ready to drown.

Which God would allow this to happen, give
many a hopeful ray
and in one moment take my baby away, what an
unbearable tease.

"Say your goodbyes now"—something that
haunts me till today.
Is it so easy? Saying bye to the next 50 years of
our life.
Give us one moment, please.

I know you suffered, and I do want to see you at
peace
just didn't know it would happen but won't leave
me in one piece.
But this isn't goodbye, I will see you soon.
Till then I'll remember, stroking your soft hair,
me singing to you, forever etched, all nights that
follow shall croon.
My mind begged "Just go already, be with the
almighty,
you already have a part of my soul"
I will see you soon my baby, it's not a wish but a
forever fact!
Guess you wanted to stay till you personally
conveyed "Mummy, I will be ok, don't be sad."
For you knew it was but just a moment of
separation.

Our moments finite, in this life destined for
partition
For I was just your conduit, helping to transition
The beeping machines gestured your departure,
cries became fainter,

as though you could sense the angelic wings
being lowered to you. From heavens up high.
And, boy, did you fly!

I will always remember our one last cuddle.
Your touch and gaze, to me, was like magic.
I wish I could bottle up your smell, everything
about you kept me in a fuddle.
Laying you down, you looked more radiant and
beautiful than ever
If only the hole could be bigger, life would no
longer be tragic.

You deserved all the happiness in the world,
I know you have gone too soon, some days I still
can't believe it's true.
How can I not feel guilty of living each day
without you?
But in our last hug, your soul whispered—"it
isn't your time yet…
We are destined to be together after this moment
of separation."

Raising my arms every night to feel you give me
a hug,
just knowing your soul might.
Longing to be engulfed in the warmth of
memories,
in the moments I held you tight.

Life is fleeting, separations are constant and in
the end you're only left with stories.

How to be your mother, that's all I know.
You clutching my finger and looking into my
eyes
"It's ok mummy, it's just not our time."
Even if it takes a thousand deaths to be with you
It's only a moment of separation for our two
souls.

Come to me my baby, for I am not as strong as
you
The brightness has gone in life and I'm missing
the flavour too
I need you to feel complete again, I know I'm
selfish but a mother's love knows no other way.
In my mind, it's not days, weeks, months or
years to come.
It is just a moment of separation.

(0,0)

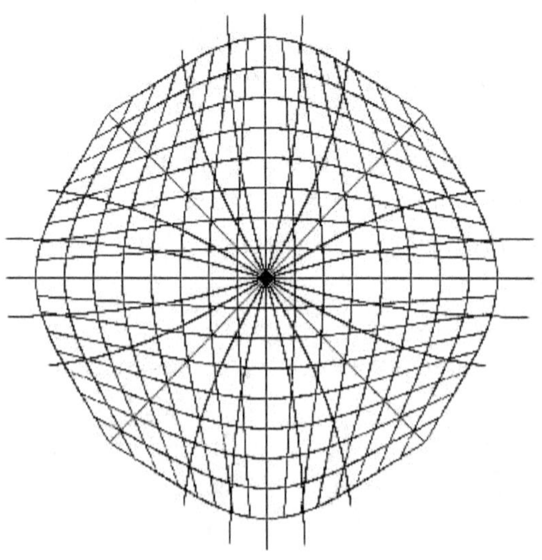

From times immemorial, since Earth was born
You and me, when we first walked and breathed
in and out,
We each do our part and then take the exit,
All puppets connected by a thread.
The one constant in our life's rhythm—the
origin

Close your eyes and imagine a sheet of graph,
You go up in life, plotting your every move, can
you hear God laugh?

If only outcomes were dependent on one axis
alone,
X being the luck and destiny
And your 'karma' being Y

Alas, how far you get on the curve depends on
your luck too
And the progress along these 2 axes is rarely
ever so linear.
You never know the break in your life's graph,
and what you will do
And, which axis will you blame for it—x or y?
Your journey is unique to you and never will be
similar.

And what exactly is (0,0)---it's your
origin—your roots
Your roots, basics in life, where everything is
simple
Quite contrary to the situation you face on the
ground
Where it's sometimes difficult to carry on in
spite of all the know how
Roots are a hidden gem, only visible to you and
available all year round.

Is there a way you can strengthen your roots
Roots have it in them to reset you.

For you may reach high on the curve only to fall
soon
You can only take a hit if your roots are spread
out and strong
Not giving enough care to where you came
from, is just wrong

The roots are there, now and forever
Even when your leaves burn out or your wings
torn
These roots become your power—your anchors
in the storm
Keeping you shielded from all seasons of life
They carry ancient wisdom of your ancestors
and ties that could never sever

Does life have a reset button?
Will it take you to your origin?
How many times can you use it?
Does rebooting yourself ever fail? So many
questions.
If only you visit roots more often, you will lose
all apprehensions.

In life, you may keep planting seeds, trying to
move forward,
forever dancing between X and Y.
Take a trip to the sacred depths anytime, not just
when you're vexed.

Your origin is what makes you, helping you
think before you sow
And in the end, it's only your roots that help you
grow.

Flow of a river called Grief

In the harshest weather, unfathomable coldness,
standing alone
Scared of what might happen, feeling the
darkness closing in,
So close, it felt palpable, with one poke at that
smoky devil—it rained hell
All over my dreams, my happiness gone with the
pellets, drowned in sorrow

This is new, and it doesn't feel true
Maybe this hasn't happened and I am just caught
in a never-ending nightmare.
Reality now changed completely, but inside I'm
clinging on to the last shred of the old me
O denial, my sweet escape—wish our furlough
never ends.

Emotions cascading rapidly, feeling like
jumping out of my skin.
Grumbling and rumbling, throwing fits,
destroying everything in sight
I plan to fight, with everything I have got,
targeting aimlessly self-destruction forerun
Anger cutting rocks and reshaping the course of
my life hereon
Slowly decelerating, I look above, dear God,
what have I done
What can I do to make the luck smile at me
again?
Is it my getting up late in the morning, I protract
and reflect
Did I not pray hard enough, mind meanders
through infinite bends and introspects.

And then it hits, pace slower than a tortoise, am
I even moving forward?
To others it may seem I am standing still.
Ironically, I'm at my deepest here, full of
wisdom and tapping into virtues unknown,
echoes of requiems running through, as an ode
to lifelessness, hope's downhill.

Nothing excites, leaves me with no desire to
flourish and cherish
Trivial chores seeming like climbing to the top,
simply to perish

Progress from a third person's angle, is as good
as none
Water so slow yet deep, infested with crocodiles,
devouring from inside.

It has been so long here, is the worst now over?
Going down the slope of emotions, merging and
dividing thoughts all along
Quietly welcoming upon a veil of shining light
over my entire being
Seeing on the surface, scars seem to have
healed, time played the magic gong

But what if this warmth too is short-lived?
Will I be made to go through it all again, I have
just found my solid ground.
And know in my heart, what I am capable of,
just in case.
Should I fear this broad and endless horizon,
terrors surround.

Feels like I have lived my waxes and wanes,
Ready to merge and surrender guided by the
Holy son.
Of all the things this journey of woe has taught
me,
handling grief with poise and vigour would be
my takeaway number one.

The unsung Hero

Loss hits everyone distinctively,
People commended for their boldness,
It's not expected for a mother to be so strong
And for a dad, "man up", "provide" and "look
after the broken mom."

An empty cradle telling a story that is forever
hushed,
a father's grieving journey has been endlessly
rushed.
He too had dreams, hopes, his legacy to share,
"Give her all the time to heal" and for him rarely
anyone to care.

By night, his guise wearing off, cape tattered and
torn.

Silently picking up the pieces, repairing with
sweat and tears
Even though his life has gone up in flames,
He gets up next morning, strives to conquer his
fears.

A million thoughts etched forever in mind,
optimism playing foul.
Echoes of laughter replaced by ringing howls
Helpless and scared, a mountain of tasks to be
finished by dawn.
And no slacking there, life goes on

A future that he envisioned, oh-so-proudly,
suddenly comes to a staggering halt.
Often finds himself walking alone with thoughts,
in a futile attempt to find any solace of sorts.

Tears are meant to fall, but are they meant to be
seen?
Only living in the shadow of memories, never
easy it has been.
Bound by the shackles of how you should
behave
World is seldom patient with the lost soul of a
dad.

Between unspoken prayers and wishes for his
late child

he moves on, trying to balance what he has left.
The world sees him with indifference and ordinarily,
judging by what he is meant to do customarily.

Somewhere in the background, Dad's broken spirit lurks
Donning a tough exterior going about life, like his angel never existed.
Unbeknownst to the world, his angel is happily put in his hero's heart
For there he will be the most shielded and they'd never part.

Nature's There

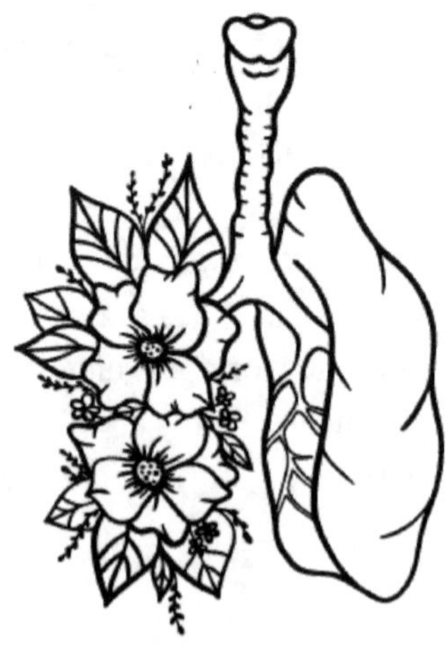

Open your window, let the breeze flow in
And air out your heart's perturbations
Feel the warmth of the sun rejuvenate your eyes.
Seems they had been crying since last night

On a tree, spot the birds trying to build a nest,
Flying to and fro carrying small twigs towards
their dream
Chirping and flapping their tiny wings, doing
their best
One last addition and they're almost done, a
formidable team.

Circling the tree the cat eyes the bird's sanctuary
Three lovely eggs, what an easy catch
Flowers in the garden take stock, amidst mute
commentary
Sometimes just leave it to God, if it's meant to
be the eggs will hatch.

The ears don't miss the stream's prattle
This white noise puts you in a trance
While happy birds on the tree do their dance
Unaware of the danger that lies ahead, for the
evening they settle.
Nature always finds a way to strike balance,
what goes up, must come down.
It can be ferocious and mellow, loud and calm,
can scare you and also act like a clown.
The cat walking on the dry leaves creating a
symphony
The crickets humming along croaking away to
glory, proudly contributing to the cacophony.

Cat weaves a scheme, supper will be deviled
eggs.
One jump and on the tree trunk, silently closing
in on the bird's nest
Suddenly the sky looks somber, as though
waiting to take the cat down a peg
And clouds burst with tears of laughter, mocking
cat's plan

And the cat slips and hits the ground, taken
aback by nature's ploy
Bird's family lives to see another day,
overflowing with joy
failure is everywhere in nature, but so is
resilience wherever you go.
So much to learn and heal, you just need to open
your window,

Beneath the big blue sky, nature takes all under
its wings
Each element has a virtue that we must imbibe
Be it the mountains or the forests, the sun or the
sand
They all show us how to live, just have to give
your hand.

One day with You

If we could go back in time and change it, I will
pick one day with you
Once again to hold you close, my heart wanting
to live what it yearns

Break of dawn, eyes half open, glare gently
waking us up,
making most of our cuddles, sharing the same
air, feeling unreal.

Smiles on our faces, we talk about how we want
to spend our day
Do we go to the park or the mall or laze around
at home, whatever you say?

Making our favourite meal, we sit together breaking bread,
Your every bite satiating my stomach, feeling carved forever in my head.

I get you ready, pick out your favourite colours and prints
You smile at me, and I already can't wait for you to have the best time

Out the door, it's all ours to explore, our giggles echoing all around.
Driving here and there, world passing by, while you fixate on clouds.

Taking you to the beach, seeing you playing with sand,
We feel the wind in our hair, and enjoy the sight of boats setting sail.

Me seeing the same old things, but it's from a different eye
God only knows how much I have longed for this joy

Like best friends reading each other's minds, moving from one activity to next
Time passing so fast, seems like hours flying by, hard to describe in text.

We go to the mountains, chasing butterflies
Jumping in and out of puddles, we leave our
footprints together

We build a fire and I tell you all the stories I can
think of,
Make animals from shadows and all the yummy
fruits we scoff

Trying foolishly to put all years worth of effort
and fun into one day
But, for you and this irrevocable desire—I will
do it all and do it all again.

Come nightfall, we enjoy nature's lullaby while
lying on the cool grass
Your hand in mine, you stare in awe of the night
sky and a million twinkling stars

Your company is intoxicating, heart knowing it's
almost too good to be true
It's like you're the drug and, now I cannot
imagine any day without you

The earth may stop spinning, it can be the end of
time and winter may come and go
But a day with you will always be my sacred
haunt, where I will be frequently running to.

A Mother's Heart

Working like clockwork, juggling a million
things simultaneously
Complaining and fretting to all, practically
functioning on no sleep
But take away all the chores from her, what are
you left with?
A heart that wants to do more, on her own terms,
for her family.
Talking about it all the time—is an add-on she
enjoys.

Vast and deeper than any ocean, not just here,
the entire solar system
Her mind full of dreams, wishes and love, can
accommodate 1000 lives.
She knows not what's extreme and can give
selflessly her heart, body and soul

Her armoury has an unlimited stash of hugs and
kisses, the most lethal cure for any woe.
Hands are no less magic, and can nurture you
well, making sure nothing deprives.

Everything she does, wears a bright smile,
hiding the weariness inside
For her family, her strength becomes 10x in
times of obligation
She will cry for you and be happier than you in
your times of glee
Such is her demeanour, not showing what she
doesn't want you to see.
While you take one step at a time, she's already
leapt 10x, no matter the situation

Her love in the purest form, it's the only love
where she expects nothing in return
The reservoir of warmth keeps bubbling
persistently, never goes empty
Always managing your moods for her wishes
she always has to adjourn
God gives her a tad more energy and strength, so
she can show her best self
You may like her more or less but her love for
you is constant

A love so strong that even Gods think twice to
come in between

A love that has the power to heal all wounds
however mean
And wielding a heart that has the power to hold
all her children, a pillar for all to lean
It may not win everyday but doesn't give up so
easily in the face of a scare
You can always count on it for anything, she will
take the utmost care.

The busier the mother's heart, fuller is her life,
After a while, success isn't measured in terms of
how much she makes
But how many lives she has taught how to earn
Her wealth not measured in terms of the number
of jewels she owns
But by her children's happiness and health

In all the stormy nights, her love keeps everyone
sure-footed
Keeping your needs before her, day, evening or
rain,
A mother's heart forever hiding sacrifices, toils
in and out, you're her main
Her luxury is in simple things in life, you only
have to treat her right
Her dreams, only a fragment of her imagination,
living vicariously through her children every
night.

Whatever floats your boat

Eyes closed, what do you see, is it peace or the
next thing you have to complete
It can be anything you want to do, mind just
wants to be set free
The shackles of your circumstance, limiting your
horizon
Feeding off the negativity, killing all the fun

Try try till you see the light, can be any colour
you want
Focus your mind with all your might, don't let
the world around daunt
Must be the last thing you'd want to do
Chant with me 1, 2, 3 'Omm...'

If chanting is not your style, then figure out what
gets you grounded

What makes you smile inside and happy for
others, less bothered
Is it dance or singing or playing a sport or
cooking or things less cluttered.
Do whatever that floats your boat, being
balanced is the ultimate g.o.a.t

What's in these techniques that makes us calm
Setting off a frequency, you feel like you can
glide across realms.
It's absolutely free of cost, just be disciplined
there is no other pre-condition
Rich, poor all can join, the same technique, it's a
race to finish for salvation.

Only you are in command of your happiness,
and it has to come from within,
not dependent on anyone else, that's the magic of
it all
labyrinth of hardships will be ever-present, don't
sit and wait for a djinn
Centre your mind, the approach will definitely
work if you're in it for the long-haul

So go on try this spiritual purging, relax your
mental grind
Be more mindfully available to your near and
dear ones.
What exercise is to body; meditation is to mind

One useless without the other, combined they
have a power of 1000 suns.

Change being the only constant, you can fool
your mind into perpetual happiness
Be there for the people you care
Just sleeping over chaos won't get you there
Today, altering your karma for cleaner thoughts,
is the new radness.

Cannot control destiny but only your karma
Go to a plane, where the heart and soul align
Now close your eyes again, what do you see?
Past all the pandemonium,
Finally, you are able to summit the quietude and
it feels like home!

Every Time

"What a good mother you are
Looks like you know what you're doing"
Each time I hear this,
It makes me think of you and how I could've
been better.

Every time I see my family and friends being
kind to me
It makes me think of you, how they'd love and
spoil you too if only you were here.

Every time I see anything beautiful in nature
It makes me think of you, how amazed you
would've been and the beauty for me would then
increase exponentially.

Every time I hear a melody soothing to my soul
It makes me think of you, how we could've
gotten lost and grooved to the rhythm…

Every time I eat something I love
I wonder would you have liked it too?

Every time I hug my first-born...
It makes me think of you
Would your body feel the same as his?

Every time I hear about miracles
It makes me think of you...
If God should've been kinder to us.

Every time I breathe
It makes me think of you
How you've used up all your breaths
And left us behind in despair of unknown
depths.

But, every time I look up and see the stars and
moon
I am content 'cause I just know wherever you
are, you see them too.

Everything I do makes me think of you.

Echoes of Carnage

Time passes, and life bulletins change
You're taught to only move forward
To outrun the shadows or be forever deranged
When is a good time to reminisce about what
you lost?

Can you return to the battlefield unscathed?
Where it all went down
Where your life's course was eternally altered.
Picture it mentally first, abort mission the
second you start to frown.

More time passes, you feel ready
Not memories alone can make you heavy
Rolling up your sleeves, marching with vigour
Carrying past memories as your ammo

Reaching the spot, flooded with memories
Mind slowly losing the grasp of reality
Brain no longer trusting what the eyes can see
For it is conjuring instances of its own

What made you believe you were ready?!
Losing your sense of purpose,
Now just focus on getting yourself together.
You expose yourself on the frontline.

Like taking a bullet, no blood spattered but pain
equally real
Mouth absolutely sewn shut but can hear your
own scream
Your loss and grief have just manifested
themselves
So real you can almost touch them

Distancing yourself from the ordeal
Back to the warmth and support of your loved
ones
Thinking about the terror you faced, there's no
way to triumph.
Away from the scene but still closer to the
echoes.

The Stallion and the River

Look at the river, a stallion stands
Tall and proud, right in the middle of the choppy
waters
High in spirits and strength in hands

With a mane like fire he charges the water
"Make way for me, let me cross," he snorts
But the mighty river doesn't bother

Waves crashing against his foot, trying hard to
displace
"Should I go back, seems the universe is plotting
against me," he thinks
Lifting his limbs, he decides to face the foe with
grace.

With each stride, he fights the tide
Waves now bowing down to his prowess
Hopes and dreams alive he emerges victorious
on the other side.

Amidst life's many tributaries, no matter how
wild and wide
Live each moment and experience the ebbs and
flows
For these waves are only crossed by those who
dare to ride.

The lone Elephant

Under the sky vast and wide
Roams a gentle beast in plain sight
Green pastures all around but no appetite to
devour
Only finding solace reflecting in the golden
hour.

Where is its family, why is it alone?
Aren't elephants social creatures
Much like men, they thrive in groups
Like everyone in a quest for their troops.

A breeze travels from far whispers into its wise
ears
"Go be with your herd, they haven't seen you in
all these years."
The elephant trumpets and lets out a sigh

"Some healings are meant to happen alone, don't
ask me why."

The elephant walks miles, introspecting
His silence speaks volumes, shadows dance
where his foot falls
In his soul, a longing remains
The forest paths might have changed, but he
knows he will still find a way.

Colours of Nature

Steel grey skies enveloping the tangerine setting
sun,
the lush greens swaying from one side to the
other,
with the ever-increasing cloudiness of the grey
floating masses

One's heart just fills with hope,
hoping to see those colourless pearls drop from
above
Mother Nature has a way of leading you on

These precious pearls will not only quench the
thirst of the earthly beings but also alleviate the
terrain of our earth!

But lo as if the powerful skies have chalked out
a different plan,
together they rumble and grumble forming the
most exquisite shining light that one can ever
see

This bolt of lightning has the capacity to scare,
to annihilate.
It feels as if anything is possible in that moment,
your dreams, hopes and even the worst fears.
Minutes later there is silence that prevails,
followed by a massive downpour!
Finally, it rains!
There is something very calming about the
petrichor…

The trees dance to the music of falling droplets
throughout the night,
as though celebrating the rain's victory over the
presently faded moon.

Dawn breaks a few hours later and with that
emerges a gigantic bright yellow mass brimming
with warmth.
It seems to be engulfing each corner;

Wet green grass turns golden as though inflicted
with Midas's touch!

That one last drop drips from the leaf,
reminiscing its past glory.

Nature has a rainbow of hues in its kitty and not
just in the way it appears
but also in the way it portrays itself every minute
each day, as such.

We're just lucky to witness these wonders
everyday
A similar story we too find in life, with elements
identical
Our journey goes on with each passing storm,
they say.
One should just look around and appreciate its
stupefying miracle.

www.ingramcontent.com/pod-product-compliance
Lightning Source LLC
La Vergne TN
LVHW050920200726
843508LV00011B/2243